With Love and Fondest Memories of:

HONORING

Ms. Bee

Broken Family Chain Poem

I little knew that morning; God was going to call your name.
In life I loved you dearly, in death I do the same.

It broke my heart to lose you. You did not go alone
for part of me went with you, the day God called you home.

You left me beautiful memories; your love is still my guide
and though we cannot see you,
you're always at my side.

Our family chain is broken and nothing seems the same
but as God calls us one by one, the chain will link again.

~ Ron Tranmer

My support system includes:

_____

_____

_____

_____

_____

_____

_____

_____

_____

_____

_____

_____

_____

_____

_____

_____

_____

_____

_____

I remember...

_____

_____

_____

_____

_____

_____

_____

_____

_____

_____

_____

_____

_____

_____

_____

_____

Remembering you is easy, I do it every day.
Missing you is the heartache that never goes
away. ~ Saying Goodbye.org

I remember…

I remember...

_____

_____

_____

_____

_____

_____

_____

_____

_____

_____

_____

_____

_____

_____

_____

_____

HONORING
Ms. Bee

I remember...

_____

_____

_____

_____

_____

_____

_____

_____

_____

_____

_____

_____

_____

_____

_____

_____

_____

_____

_____

I remember...

_____

_____

_____

_____

_____

_____

_____

_____

_____

_____

_____

_____

_____

_____

_____

_____

_____

_____

_____

_____

_____

I remember...

_____

_____

_____

_____

_____

_____

_____

_____

_____

_____

_____

_____

_____

_____

_____

_____

_____

_____

_____

_____

_____

_____

I'm thinking and feeling...

_____

_____

_____

_____

_____

_____

_____

_____

_____

_____

_____

_____

_____

_____

_____

_____

Be the things you loved most about your
loved one who is gone. ~UNKNOWN

I'm thinking and feeling...

_____

_____

_____

_____

_____

_____

_____

_____

_____

_____

_____

_____

_____

_____

_____

_____

_____

_____

_____

I'm thinking and feeling...

_____

_____

_____

_____

_____

_____

_____

_____

_____

_____

_____

_____

_____

_____

_____

_____

_____

_____

_____

HONORING

Ms. Bee

I'm thinking and feeling...

I'm thinking and feeling...

_____

_____

_____

_____

_____

_____

_____

_____

_____

_____

_____

_____

_____

_____

_____

_____

HONORING
Ms. Bee

Date: /   /

If I need support today, I can call:

_____

My plans for today include:

_____

_____

_____

Today, I'm really missing:

Today I:
☐ Feel supported
☐ Feel angry
☐ Feel like crying
☐ Feel tired
☐ Feel sad
☐ Feel neutral
☐ Am taking it minute by minute

_____

_____

_____

If you were here, I would tell you: _____

_____

_____

I find it helpful when: _____

_____

_____

_____

I am comforted by: _____

_____

_____

_____

_____

I feel your presence most when: _____

_____

_____

Date: /   /

If I need support today, I can call:

_____

My plans for today include:

_____

_____

_____

Today, I'm really missing:

Today I:
☐ Feel supported
☐ Feel angry
☐ Feel like crying
☐ Feel tired
☐ Feel sad
☐ Feel neutral
☐ Am taking it minute by minute

_____

_____

_____

If you were here, I would tell you: _____

_____

_____

I find it helpful when: _____

_____

_____

_____

I am comforted by: _____

_____

_____

_____

I feel your presence most when: _____

_____

_____

Date: /   /

If I need support today, I can call:

_____

My plans for today include:

_____

_____

_____

Today, I'm really missing:

Today I:
- ☐ Feel supported
- ☐ Feel angry
- ☐ Feel like crying
- ☐ Feel tired
- ☐ Feel sad
- ☐ Feel neutral
- ☐ Am taking it minute by minute

_____

_____

_____

If you were here, I would tell you: _____

_____

_____

I find it helpful when: _____

_____

_____

_____

I am comforted by: _____

_____

_____

_____

_____

I feel your presence most when: _____

_____

_____

18

Date: /   /

If I need support today, I can call:

_____

My plans for today include:

_____

_____

_____

Today, I'm really missing:

Today I:
- ☐ Feel supported
- ☐ Feel angry
- ☐ Feel like crying
- ☐ Feel tired
- ☐ Feel sad
- ☐ Feel neutral
- ☐ Am taking it minute by minute

_____

_____

_____

If you were here, I would tell you: _____

_____

_____

I find it helpful when: _____

_____

_____

_____

I am comforted by: _____

_____

_____

_____

_____

I feel your presence most when: _____

_____

_____

Date: /   /

If I need support today, I can call:

_____

My plans for today include:

_____

_____

_____

Today, I'm really missing:

Today I:
- ☐ Feel supported
- ☐ Feel angry
- ☐ Feel like crying
- ☐ Feel tired
- ☐ Feel sad
- ☐ Feel neutral
- ☐ Am taking it minute by minute

_____

_____

_____

If you were here, I would tell you: _____

_____

_____

I find it helpful when: _____

_____

_____

_____

I am comforted by: _____

_____

_____

_____

_____

I feel your presence most when: _____

_____

_____

Date: /   /

If I need support today, I can call:

_____

My plans for today include:

_____

_____

_____

Today, I'm really missing:

Today I:
☐ Feel supported
☐ Feel angry
☐ Feel like crying
☐ Feel tired
☐ Feel sad
☐ Feel neutral
☐ Am taking it minute by minute

_____

_____

_____

If you were here, I would tell you: _____

_____

I find it helpful when: _____

_____

_____

I am comforted by: _____

_____

_____

_____

I feel your presence most when: _____

_____

_____

Date: /   /

If I need support today, I can call:

_____

My plans for today include:

_____

_____

_____

Today, I'm really missing:

Today I:
☐ Feel supported
☐ Feel angry
☐ Feel like crying
☐ Feel tired
☐ Feel sad
☐ Feel neutral
☐ Am taking it minute by minute

_____

_____

_____

If you were here, I would tell you: _____

_____

_____

I find it helpful when: _____

_____

_____

_____

I am comforted by: _____

_____

_____

_____

I feel your presence most when: _____

_____

_____

Date: /   /

If I need support today, I can call:

_____

My plans for today include:

_____

_____

_____

Today, I'm really missing:

_____

_____

_____

If you were here, I would tell you: _____

_____

_____

I find it helpful when: _____

_____

_____

_____

I am comforted by: _____

_____

_____

_____

_____

I feel your presence most when: _____

_____

_____

Today I:
☐ Feel supported
☐ Feel angry
☐ Feel like crying
☐ Feel tired
☐ Feel sad
☐ Feel neutral
☐ Am taking it minute by minute

Date: / /

If I need support today, I can call:

_____

My plans for today include:

_____

_____

_____

Today, I'm really missing:

Today I:
- ☐ Feel supported
- ☐ Feel angry
- ☐ Feel like crying
- ☐ Feel tired
- ☐ Feel sad
- ☐ Feel neutral
- ☐ Am taking it minute by minute

_____

_____

_____

If you were here, I would tell you: _____

_____

I find it helpful when: _____

_____

_____

I am comforted by: _____

_____

_____

_____

I feel your presence most when: _____

_____

_____

Date: /   /

If I need support today, I can call:

_____

My plans for today include:

_____

_____

_____

Today, I'm really missing:

Today I:
☐ Feel supported
☐ Feel angry
☐ Feel like crying
☐ Feel tired
☐ Feel sad
☐ Feel neutral
☐ Am taking it
minute by minute

_____

_____

_____

If you were here, I would tell you: _____

_____

_____

I find it helpful when: _____

_____

_____

_____

I am comforted by: _____

_____

_____

_____

_____

I feel your presence most when: _____

_____

_____

Date: / /

If I need support today, I can call:

_____

My plans for today include:

_____

_____

_____

Today, I'm really missing:

_____

_____

_____

If you were here, I would tell you: _____

_____

I find it helpful when: _____

_____

_____

I am comforted by: _____

_____

_____

_____

I feel your presence most when: _____

_____

_____

Today I:
- ☐ Feel supported
- ☐ Feel angry
- ☐ Feel like crying
- ☐ Feel tired
- ☐ Feel sad
- ☐ Feel neutral
- ☐ Am taking it minute by minute

Date: /   /

If I need support today, I can call:

_____

My plans for today include:

_____

_____

_____

Today, I'm really missing:

_____

_____

_____

If you were here, I would tell you: _____

_____

_____

I find it helpful when: _____

_____

_____

_____

I am comforted by: _____

_____

_____

_____

_____

I feel your presence most when: _____

_____

_____

Date: /   /

If I need support today, I can call:

_____

My plans for today include:

_____

_____

_____

Today, I'm really missing:

_____

_____

_____

If you were here, I would tell you: _____

_____

I find it helpful when: _____

_____

_____

I am comforted by: _____

_____

_____

_____

I feel your presence most when: _____

_____

_____

Today I:
☐ Feel supported
☐ Feel angry
☐ Feel like crying
☐ Feel tired
☐ Feel sad
☐ Feel neutral
☐ Am taking it minute by minute

Date: / /

If I need support today, I can call:

_____

My plans for today include:

_____

_____

_____

Today, I'm really missing:

Today I:
☐ Feel supported
☐ Feel angry
☐ Feel like crying
☐ Feel tired
☐ Feel sad
☐ Feel neutral
☐ Am taking it minute by minute

_____

_____

_____

If you were here, I would tell you: _____

_____

_____

I find it helpful when: _____

_____

_____

_____

I am comforted by: _____

_____

_____

_____

_____

I feel your presence most when: _____

_____

_____

Date: ___ / ___ / ___

If I need support today, I can call:

_____

My plans for today include:

_____

_____

_____

Today, I'm really missing:

Today I:
- ☐ Feel supported
- ☐ Feel angry
- ☐ Feel like crying
- ☐ Feel tired
- ☐ Feel sad
- ☐ Feel neutral
- ☐ Am taking it minute by minute

_____

_____

_____

If you were here, I would tell you: _____

_____

_____

I find it helpful when: _____

_____

_____

_____

I am comforted by: _____

_____

_____

_____

_____

I feel your presence most when: _____

_____

_____

Date: /   /

If I need support today, I can call:

_____

My plans for today include:

_____

_____

_____

Today, I'm really missing:

Today I:
- ☐ Feel supported
- ☐ Feel angry
- ☐ Feel like crying
- ☐ Feel tired
- ☐ Feel sad
- ☐ Feel neutral
- ☐ Am taking it minute by minute

_____

_____

_____

If you were here, I would tell you: _____

_____

_____

I find it helpful when: _____

_____

_____

_____

I am comforted by: _____

_____

_____

_____

_____

I feel your presence most when: _____

_____

_____

Date: /   /

If I need support today, I can call:

_____

My plans for today include:

_____

_____

_____

Today, I'm really missing:

_____

_____

_____

If you were here, I would tell you: _____

_____

_____

I find it helpful when: _____

_____

_____

_____

I am comforted by: _____

_____

_____

_____

_____

I feel your presence most when: _____

_____

_____

Date: /   /

If I need support today, I can call:

_____

My plans for today include:

_____

_____

_____

Today, I'm really missing:

Today I:
- ☐ Feel supported
- ☐ Feel angry
- ☐ Feel like crying
- ☐ Feel tired
- ☐ Feel sad
- ☐ Feel neutral
- ☐ Am taking it minute by minute

_____

_____

_____

If you were here, I would tell you: _____

_____

_____

I find it helpful when: _____

_____

_____

_____

I am comforted by: _____

_____

_____

_____

_____

I feel your presence most when: _____

_____

_____

Date: /   /

If I need support today, I can call:

_____

My plans for today include:

_____

_____

_____

Today, I'm really missing:

Today I:
☐ Feel supported
☐ Feel angry
☐ Feel like crying
☐ Feel tired
☐ Feel sad
☐ Feel neutral
☐ Am taking it minute by minute

_____

_____

_____

If you were here, I would tell you: _____

_____

_____

I find it helpful when: _____

_____

_____

_____

I am comforted by: _____

_____

_____

_____

_____

I feel your presence most when: _____

_____

_____

Date: /   /

If I need support today, I can call:

_____

My plans for today include:

_____

_____

_____

Today, I'm really missing:

<table>
<tr><td>Today I:</td></tr>
<tr><td>☐ Feel supported</td></tr>
<tr><td>☐ Feel angry</td></tr>
<tr><td>☐ Feel like crying</td></tr>
<tr><td>☐ Feel tired</td></tr>
<tr><td>☐ Feel sad</td></tr>
<tr><td>☐ Feel neutral</td></tr>
<tr><td>☐ Am taking it minute by minute</td></tr>
</table>

_____

_____

_____

If you were here, I would tell you: _____

_____

_____

I find it helpful when: _____

_____

_____

_____

I am comforted by: _____

_____

_____

_____

I feel your presence most when: _____

_____

_____

Date: / /

If I need support today, I can call:

_____

My plans for today include:

_____

_____

_____

Today, I'm really missing:

Today I:
☐ Feel supported
☐ Feel angry
☐ Feel like crying
☐ Feel tired
☐ Feel sad
☐ Feel neutral
☐ Am taking it minute by minute

_____

_____

_____

If you were here, I would tell you: _____

_____

_____

I find it helpful when: _____

_____

_____

_____

I am comforted by: _____

_____

_____

_____

_____

I feel your presence most when: _____

_____

_____

Date: /   /

If I need support today, I can call:

_____

My plans for today include:

_____

_____

_____

Today, I'm really missing:

Today I:
☐ Feel supported
☐ Feel angry
☐ Feel like crying
☐ Feel tired
☐ Feel sad
☐ Feel neutral
☐ Am taking it minute by minute

_____

_____

_____

If you were here, I would tell you: _____

_____

_____

I find it helpful when: _____

_____

_____

_____

I am comforted by: _____

_____

_____

_____

_____

I feel your presence most when: _____

_____

_____

Date: ___ / ___ / ___

If I need support today, I can call:

_____

My plans for today include:

_____

_____

_____

Today, I'm really missing:

_____

_____

_____

If you were here, I would tell you: _____

_____

_____

I find it helpful when: _____

_____

_____

_____

I am comforted by: _____

_____

_____

_____

_____

I feel your presence most when: _____

_____

_____

Today I:
- ☐ Feel supported
- ☐ Feel angry
- ☐ Feel like crying
- ☐ Feel tired
- ☐ Feel sad
- ☐ Feel neutral
- ☐ Am taking it minute by minute

Date: /   /

If I need support today, I can call:

_____

My plans for today include:

_____

_____

_____

Today, I'm really missing:

Today I:
☐ Feel supported
☐ Feel angry
☐ Feel like crying
☐ Feel tired
☐ Feel sad
☐ Feel neutral
☐ Am taking it minute by minute

_____

_____

_____

If you were here, I would tell you: _____

_____

_____

I find it helpful when: _____

_____

_____

_____

I am comforted by: _____

_____

_____

_____

I feel your presence most when: _____

_____

_____

39

Date: /   /

If I need support today, I can call:

_____

My plans for today include:

_____

_____

_____

Today, I'm really missing:

Today I:
☐ Feel supported
☐ Feel angry
☐ Feel like crying
☐ Feel tired
☐ Feel sad
☐ Feel neutral
☐ Am taking it minute by minute

_____

_____

_____

If you were here, I would tell you: _____

_____

_____

I find it helpful when: _____

_____

_____

_____

I am comforted by: _____

_____

_____

_____

_____

I feel your presence most when: _____

_____

_____

Date: /   /

If I need support today, I can call:

_____

My plans for today include:

_____

_____

_____

Today, I'm really missing:

Today I:
☐ Feel supported
☐ Feel angry
☐ Feel like crying
☐ Feel tired
☐ Feel sad
☐ Feel neutral
☐ Am taking it minute by minute

_____

_____

_____

If you were here, I would tell you: _____

_____

_____

I find it helpful when: _____

_____

_____

_____

I am comforted by: _____

_____

_____

_____

_____

I feel your presence most when: _____

_____

_____

41

Date: /   /

If I need support today, I can call:

_____

My plans for today include:

_____

_____

_____

Today, I'm really missing:

Today I:
☐ Feel supported
☐ Feel angry
☐ Feel like crying
☐ Feel tired
☐ Feel sad
☐ Feel neutral
☐ Am taking it minute by minute

_____

_____

_____

If you were here, I would tell you: _____

_____

_____

I find it helpful when: _____

_____

_____

_____

I am comforted by: _____

_____

_____

_____

_____

I feel your presence most when: _____

_____

_____

Date: /   /

If I need support today, I can call:

_____

My plans for today include:

_____

_____

_____

Today, I'm really missing:

Today I:
☐ Feel supported
☐ Feel angry
☐ Feel like crying
☐ Feel tired
☐ Feel sad
☐ Feel neutral
☐ Am taking it minute by minute

_____

_____

_____

If you were here, I would tell you: _____

_____

_____

I find it helpful when: _____

_____

_____

_____

I am comforted by: _____

_____

_____

_____

_____

I feel your presence most when: _____

_____

_____

Date: ___ / ___ / ___

If I need support today, I can call:

_____

My plans for today include:

_____

_____

_____

Today, I'm really missing:

Today I:
- ☐ Feel supported
- ☐ Feel angry
- ☐ Feel like crying
- ☐ Feel tired
- ☐ Feel sad
- ☐ Feel neutral
- ☐ Am taking it minute by minute

_____

_____

_____

If you were here, I would tell you: _____

_____

_____

I find it helpful when: _____

_____

_____

_____

I am comforted by: _____

_____

_____

_____

_____

I feel your presence most when: _____

_____

_____

Date: /   /

If I need support today, I can call:

_____

My plans for today include:

_____

_____

_____

Today, I'm really missing:

_____

_____

_____

If you were here, I would tell you: _____

_____

_____

I find it helpful when: _____

_____

_____

_____

I am comforted by: _____

_____

_____

_____

_____

I feel your presence most when: _____

_____

_____

Date: ___ / ___ / ___

If I need support today, I can call:

_____

My plans for today include:

_____

_____

_____

Today, I'm really missing:

_____

_____

_____

If you were here, I would tell you: _____

_____

_____

I find it helpful when: _____

_____

_____

_____

I am comforted by: _____

_____

_____

_____

_____

I feel your presence most when: _____

_____

_____

Today I:
☐ Feel supported
☐ Feel angry
☐ Feel like crying
☐ Feel tired
☐ Feel sad
☐ Feel neutral
☐ Am taking it minute by minute

Date: /   /

If I need support today, I can call:

_____

My plans for today include:

_____

_____

_____

Today, I'm really missing:

Today I:
☐ Feel supported
☐ Feel angry
☐ Feel like crying
☐ Feel tired
☐ Feel sad
☐ Feel neutral
☐ Am taking it minute by minute

_____

_____

_____

If you were here, I would tell you: _____

_____

_____

I find it helpful when: _____

_____

_____

_____

I am comforted by: _____

_____

_____

_____

_____

I feel your presence most when: _____

_____

_____

Date: /   /

If I need support today, I can call:

_____

My plans for today include:

_____

_____

_____

Today, I'm really missing:

_____

_____

_____

If you were here, I would tell you: _____

_____

I find it helpful when: _____

_____

_____

I am comforted by: _____

_____

_____

_____

I feel your presence most when: _____

_____

_____

Today I:
☐ Feel supported
☐ Feel angry
☐ Feel like crying
☐ Feel tired
☐ Feel sad
☐ Feel neutral
☐ Am taking it minute by minute

Date: /   /

If I need support today, I can call:

_____

My plans for today include:

_____

_____

_____

Today, I'm really missing:

_____

_____

_____

If you were here, I would tell you: _____

_____

_____

I find it helpful when: _____

_____

_____

_____

I am comforted by: _____

_____

_____

_____

_____

I feel your presence most when: _____

_____

_____

Date: __ / __ / __

If I need support today, I can call:

_____

My plans for today include:

_____

_____

_____

Today, I'm really missing:

_____

_____

_____

If you were here, I would tell you: _____

_____

_____

I find it helpful when: _____

_____

_____

_____

I am comforted by: _____

_____

_____

_____

_____

I feel your presence most when: _____

_____

_____

Today I:
☐ Feel supported
☐ Feel angry
☐ Feel like crying
☐ Feel tired
☐ Feel sad
☐ Feel neutral
☐ Am taking it minute by minute

Date: /   /

If I need support today, I can call:

_____

My plans for today include:

_____

_____

_____

Today, I'm really missing:

Today I:
☐ Feel supported
☐ Feel angry
☐ Feel like crying
☐ Feel tired
☐ Feel sad
☐ Feel neutral
☐ Am taking it
minute by minute

_____

_____

_____

If you were here, I would tell you: _____

_____

_____

I find it helpful when: _____

_____

_____

_____

I am comforted by: _____

_____

_____

_____

I feel your presence most when: _____

_____

_____

Date: / /

If I need support today, I can call:

_____

My plans for today include:

_____

_____

_____

Today, I'm really missing:

Today I:
- ☐ Feel supported
- ☐ Feel angry
- ☐ Feel like crying
- ☐ Feel tired
- ☐ Feel sad
- ☐ Feel neutral
- ☐ Am taking it minute by minute

_____

_____

_____

If you were here, I would tell you: _____

_____

_____

I find it helpful when: _____

_____

_____

_____

I am comforted by: _____

_____

_____

_____

_____

I feel your presence most when: _____

_____

_____

Date: /   /

If I need support today, I can call:

_____

My plans for today include:

_____

_____

_____

Today, I'm really missing:

_____

_____

_____

If you were here, I would tell you: _____

_____

_____

I find it helpful when: _____

_____

_____

_____

I am comforted by: _____

_____

_____

_____

I feel your presence most when: _____

_____

_____

Today I:
☐ Feel supported
☐ Feel angry
☐ Feel like crying
☐ Feel tired
☐ Feel sad
☐ Feel neutral
☐ Am taking it minute by minute

Date: /   /

If I need support today, I can call:

_____

My plans for today include:

_____

_____

_____

Today, I'm really missing:

Today I:
☐ Feel supported
☐ Feel angry
☐ Feel like crying
☐ Feel tired
☐ Feel sad
☐ Feel neutral
☐ Am taking it
minute by minute

_____

_____

_____

If you were here, I would tell you: _____

_____

_____

I find it helpful when: _____

_____

_____

_____

I am comforted by: _____

_____

_____

_____

_____

I feel your presence most when: _____

_____

_____

Date: /   /

If I need support today, I can call:

_____

My plans for today include:

_____

_____

_____

Today, I'm really missing:

☐ Feel supported
☐ Feel angry
☐ Feel like crying
☐ Feel tired
☐ Feel sad
☐ Feel neutral
☐ Am taking it minute by minute

_____

_____

_____

If you were here, I would tell you: _____

_____

_____

I find it helpful when: _____

_____

_____

_____

I am comforted by: _____

_____

_____

_____

_____

I feel your presence most when: _____

_____

_____

Date: /   /

If I need support today, I can call:

_____

My plans for today include:

_____

_____

_____

Today, I'm really missing:

_____

_____

_____

If you were here, I would tell you: _____

_____

_____

I find it helpful when: _____

_____

_____

_____

I am comforted by: _____

_____

_____

_____

_____

I feel your presence most when: _____

_____

_____

Today I:
- ☐ Feel supported
- ☐ Feel angry
- ☐ Feel like crying
- ☐ Feel tired
- ☐ Feel sad
- ☐ Feel neutral
- ☐ Am taking it minute by minute

Date: /   /

If I need support today, I can call:

_____

My plans for today include:

_____

_____

_____

Today, I'm really missing:

Today I:
☐ Feel supported
☐ Feel angry
☐ Feel like crying
☐ Feel tired
☐ Feel sad
☐ Feel neutral
☐ Am taking it minute by minute

_____

_____

_____

If you were here, I would tell you: _____

_____

_____

I find it helpful when: _____

_____

_____

_____

I am comforted by: _____

_____

_____

_____

_____

I feel your presence most when: _____

_____

_____

Date: / /

If I need support today, I can call:

_____

My plans for today include:

_____

_____

_____

Today, I'm really missing:

_____

_____

_____

If you were here, I would tell you: _____

_____

_____

I find it helpful when: _____

_____

_____

_____

I am comforted by: _____

_____

_____

_____

_____

I feel your presence most when: _____

_____

_____

Today I:
☐ Feel supported
☐ Feel angry
☐ Feel like crying
☐ Feel tired
☐ Feel sad
☐ Feel neutral
☐ Am taking it minute by minute

Date: /   /

If I need support today, I can call:

_____

My plans for today include:

_____

_____

_____

Today, I'm really missing:

Today I:
☐ Feel supported
☐ Feel angry
☐ Feel like crying
☐ Feel tired
☐ Feel sad
☐ Feel neutral
☐ Am taking it
minute by minute

_____

_____

_____

If you were here, I would tell you: _____

_____

I find it helpful when: _____

_____

_____

I am comforted by: _____

_____

_____

_____

I feel your presence most when: _____

_____

_____

Date: /   /

If I need support today, I can call:

_____

My plans for today include:

_____

_____

_____

Today, I'm really missing:

Today I:
- ☐ Feel supported
- ☐ Feel angry
- ☐ Feel like crying
- ☐ Feel tired
- ☐ Feel sad
- ☐ Feel neutral
- ☐ Am taking it minute by minute

_____

_____

_____

If you were here, I would tell you: _____

_____

I find it helpful when: _____

_____

_____

I am comforted by: _____

_____

_____

_____

I feel your presence most when: _____

_____

_____

Date: /   /

If I need support today, I can call:

_____

My plans for today include:

_____

_____

_____

Today, I'm really missing:

Today I:
☐ Feel supported
☐ Feel angry
☐ Feel like crying
☐ Feel tired
☐ Feel sad
☐ Feel neutral
☐ Am taking it minute by minute

_____

_____

_____

If you were here, I would tell you: _____

_____

_____

I find it helpful when: _____

_____

_____

_____

I am comforted by: _____

_____

_____

_____

I feel your presence most when: _____

_____

_____

Date: /   /

If I need support today, I can call:

_____

My plans for today include:

_____

_____

_____

Today, I'm really missing:

_____

_____

_____

If you were here, I would tell you: _____

_____

_____

I find it helpful when: _____

_____

_____

_____

I am comforted by: _____

_____

_____

_____

_____

I feel your presence most when: _____

_____

_____

Today I:
- ☐ Feel supported
- ☐ Feel angry
- ☐ Feel like crying
- ☐ Feel tired
- ☐ Feel sad
- ☐ Feel neutral
- ☐ Am taking it minute by minute

Date: /   /

If I need support today, I can call:

_____

My plans for today include:

_____

_____

_____

Today, I'm really missing:

Today I:
☐ Feel supported
☐ Feel angry
☐ Feel like crying
☐ Feel tired
☐ Feel sad
☐ Feel neutral
☐ Am taking it minute by minute

_____

_____

_____

If you were here, I would tell you: _____

_____

_____

I find it helpful when: _____

_____

_____

_____

I am comforted by: _____

_____

_____

_____

_____

I feel your presence most when: _____

_____

_____

Date: /   /

If I need support today, I can call:

_____

My plans for today include:

_____

_____

_____

Today, I'm really missing:

_____

_____

_____

If you were here, I would tell you: _____

_____

_____

I find it helpful when: _____

_____

_____

_____

I am comforted by: _____

_____

_____

_____

_____

I feel your presence most when: _____

_____

_____

Today I:
☐ Feel supported
☐ Feel angry
☐ Feel like crying
☐ Feel tired
☐ Feel sad
☐ Feel neutral
☐ Am taking it minute by minute

Date: /   /

If I need support today, I can call:

_____

My plans for today include:

_____

_____

_____

Today, I'm really missing:

Today I:
- ☐ Feel supported
- ☐ Feel angry
- ☐ Feel like crying
- ☐ Feel tired
- ☐ Feel sad
- ☐ Feel neutral
- ☐ Am taking it minute by minute

_____

_____

_____

If you were here, I would tell you: _____

_____

_____

I find it helpful when: _____

_____

_____

_____

I am comforted by: _____

_____

_____

_____

_____

I feel your presence most when: _____

_____

_____

Date: /   /

If I need support today, I can call:

_____

My plans for today include:

_____

_____

_____

Today, I'm really missing:

_____

_____

_____

If you were here, I would tell you: _____

_____

I find it helpful when: _____

_____

_____

I am comforted by: _____

_____

_____

_____

I feel your presence most when: _____

_____

_____

Date: /   /

If I need support today, I can call:

_____

My plans for today include:

_____

_____

_____

Today, I'm really missing:

Today I:
☐ Feel supported
☐ Feel angry
☐ Feel like crying
☐ Feel tired
☐ Feel sad
☐ Feel neutral
☐ Am taking it minute by minute

_____

_____

_____

If you were here, I would tell you: _____

_____

_____

I find it helpful when: _____

_____

_____

_____

I am comforted by: _____

_____

_____

_____

_____

I feel your presence most when: _____

_____

_____

Date: /   /

If I need support today, I can call:

_____

My plans for today include:

_____

_____

_____

Today, I'm really missing:

_____

_____

_____

If you were here, I would tell you: _____

_____

_____

I find it helpful when: _____

_____

_____

_____

I am comforted by: _____

_____

_____

_____

_____

I feel your presence most when: _____

_____

_____

Today I:
☐ Feel supported
☐ Feel angry
☐ Feel like crying
☐ Feel tired
☐ Feel sad
☐ Feel neutral
☐ Am taking it minute by minute

Date: /   /

If I need support today, I can call:

_____

My plans for today include:

_____

_____

_____

Today, I'm really missing:

Today I:
☐ Feel supported
☐ Feel angry
☐ Feel like crying
☐ Feel tired
☐ Feel sad
☐ Feel neutral
☐ Am taking it minute by minute

_____

_____

_____

If you were here, I would tell you: ·_____

_____

_____

I find it helpful when: _____

_____

_____

_____

I am comforted by: _____

_____

_____

_____

_____

I feel your presence most when: _____

_____

_____

Date: /   /

If I need support today, I can call:

_____

My plans for today include:

_____

_____

_____

Today, I'm really missing:

_____

_____

_____

If you were here, I would tell you: _____

_____

_____

I find it helpful when: _____

_____

_____

_____

I am comforted by: _____

_____

_____

_____

_____

I feel your presence most when: _____

_____

_____

Today I:
☐ Feel supported
☐ Feel angry
☐ Feel like crying
☐ Feel tired
☐ Feel sad
☐ Feel neutral
☐ Am taking it minute by minute

Date: /   /

If I need support today, I can call:

_____

My plans for today include:

_____

_____

_____

Today, I'm really missing:

Today I:

☐ Feel supported
☐ Feel angry
☐ Feel like crying
☐ Feel tired
☐ Feel sad
☐ Feel neutral
☐ Am taking it minute by minute

_____

_____

_____

If you were here, I would tell you: _____

_____

_____

I find it helpful when: _____

_____

_____

_____

I am comforted by: _____

_____

_____

_____

I feel your presence most when: _____

_____

_____

Date: /   /

If I need support today, I can call:

_____

My plans for today include:

_____

_____

_____

Today, I'm really missing:

Today I:
- ☐ Feel supported
- ☐ Feel angry
- ☐ Feel like crying
- ☐ Feel tired
- ☐ Feel sad
- ☐ Feel neutral
- ☐ Am taking it minute by minute

_____

_____

_____

If you were here, I would tell you: _____

_____

_____

I find it helpful when: _____

_____

_____

_____

I am comforted by: _____

_____

_____

_____

_____

I feel your presence most when: _____

_____

_____

Date: /   /

If I need support today, I can call:

_____

My plans for today include:

_____

_____

_____

Today, I'm really missing:

Today I:
☐ Feel supported
☐ Feel angry
☐ Feel like crying
☐ Feel tired
☐ Feel sad
☐ Feel neutral
☐ Am taking it minute by minute

_____

_____

_____

If you were here, I would tell you: _____

_____

I find it helpful when: _____

_____

_____

_____

I am comforted by: _____

_____

_____

_____

_____

I feel your presence most when: _____

_____

_____

Date: /   /

If I need support today, I can call:

_____

My plans for today include:

_____

_____

_____

Today, I'm really missing:

_____

_____

_____

If you were here, I would tell you: _____

_____

_____

I find it helpful when: _____

_____

_____

_____

I am comforted by: _____

_____

_____

_____

_____

I feel your presence most when: _____

_____

_____

Today I:
☐ Feel supported
☐ Feel angry
☐ Feel like crying
☐ Feel tired
☐ Feel sad
☐ Feel neutral
☐ Am taking it minute by minute

Date: /   /

If I need support today, I can call:

_____

My plans for today include:

_____

_____

_____

Today, I'm really missing:

Today I:
☐ Feel supported
☐ Feel angry
☐ Feel like crying
☐ Feel tired
☐ Feel sad
☐ Feel neutral
☐ Am taking it minute by minute

_____

_____

_____

If you were here, I would tell you: _____

_____

_____

I find it helpful when: _____

_____

_____

_____

I am comforted by: _____

_____

_____

_____

_____

I feel your presence most when: _____

_____

_____

Date: ___ / ___ / ___

If I need support today, I can call:

_____

My plans for today include:

_____

_____

_____

Today, I'm really missing:

_____

_____

_____

If you were here, I would tell you: _____

_____

_____

I find it helpful when: _____

_____

_____

_____

I am comforted by: _____

_____

_____

_____

_____

I feel your presence most when: _____

_____

_____

Today I:
- ☐ Feel supported
- ☐ Feel angry
- ☐ Feel like crying
- ☐ Feel tired
- ☐ Feel sad
- ☐ Feel neutral
- ☐ Am taking it minute by minute

Date: /   /

If I need support today, I can call:

_____

My plans for today include:

_____

_____

_____

Today, I'm really missing:

_____

_____

_____

If you were here, I would tell you: _____

_____

I find it helpful when: _____

_____

_____

I am comforted by: _____

_____

_____

_____

I feel your presence most when: _____

_____

_____

Date: /   /

If I need support today, I can call:

_____

My plans for today include:

_____

_____

_____

Today, I'm really missing:

_____

_____

_____

If you were here, I would tell you: _____

_____

_____

I find it helpful when: _____

_____

_____

_____

I am comforted by: _____

_____

_____

_____

_____

I feel your presence most when: _____

_____

_____

Today I:
☐ Feel supported
☐ Feel angry
☐ Feel like crying
☐ Feel tired
☐ Feel sad
☐ Feel neutral
☐ Am taking it minute by minute

Date: / /

If I need support today, I can call:

_____

My plans for today include:

_____

_____

_____

Today, I'm really missing:

Today I:
☐ Feel supported
☐ Feel angry
☐ Feel like crying
☐ Feel tired
☐ Feel sad
☐ Feel neutral
☐ Am taking it minute by minute

_____

_____

_____

If you were here, I would tell you: _____

_____

_____

I find it helpful when: _____

_____

_____

_____

I am comforted by: _____

_____

_____

_____

_____

I feel your presence most when: _____

_____

_____

Date: ___ / ___ / ___

If I need support today, I can call:

_____

My plans for today include:

_____

_____

_____

Today, I'm really missing:

Today I:
☐ Feel supported
☐ Feel angry
☐ Feel like crying
☐ Feel tired
☐ Feel sad
☐ Feel neutral
☐ Am taking it minute by minute

_____

_____

_____

If you were here, I would tell you: _____

_____

_____

I find it helpful when: _____

_____

_____

_____

I am comforted by: _____

_____

_____

_____

_____

I feel your presence most when: _____

_____

_____

Date: /   /

If I need support today, I can call:

_____

My plans for today include:

_____

_____

_____

Today, I'm really missing:

_____

_____

_____

If you were here, I would tell you: _____

_____

_____

I find it helpful when: _____

_____

_____

_____

I am comforted by: _____

_____

_____

_____

_____

I feel your presence most when: _____

_____

_____

Date: /   /

If I need support today, I can call:

_____

My plans for today include:

_____

_____

_____

Today, I'm really missing:

Today I:
☐ Feel supported
☐ Feel angry
☐ Feel like crying
☐ Feel tired
☐ Feel sad
☐ Feel neutral
☐ Am taking it minute by minute

_____

_____

_____

If you were here, I would tell you: _____

_____

_____

I find it helpful when: _____

_____

_____

_____

I am comforted by: _____

_____

_____

_____

_____

I feel your presence most when: _____

_____

_____

Date: /   /

If I need support today, I can call:

_____

My plans for today include:

_____

_____

_____

Today, I'm really missing:

_____

_____

_____

If you were here, I would tell you: _____

_____

_____

I find it helpful when: _____

_____

_____

I am comforted by: _____

_____

_____

_____

I feel your presence most when: _____

_____

_____

Today I:
☐ Feel supported
☐ Feel angry
☐ Feel like crying
☐ Feel tired
☐ Feel sad
☐ Feel neutral
☐ Am taking it minute by minute

Date: /   /

If I need support today, I can call:

_____

My plans for today include:

_____

_____

_____

Today, I'm really missing:

_____

_____

_____

If you were here, I would tell you: _____

_____

_____

I find it helpful when: _____

_____

_____

_____

I am comforted by: _____

_____

_____

_____

_____

I feel your presence most when: _____

_____

_____

Today I:
- ☐ Feel supported
- ☐ Feel angry
- ☐ Feel like crying
- ☐ Feel tired
- ☐ Feel sad
- ☐ Feel neutral
- ☐ Am taking it minute by minute

Date: /   /

If I need support today, I can call:

_____

My plans for today include:

_____

_____

_____

Today, I'm really missing:

Today I:
☐ Feel supported
☐ Feel angry
☐ Feel like crying
☐ Feel tired
☐ Feel sad
☐ Feel neutral
☐ Am taking it minute by minute

_____

_____

_____

If you were here, I would tell you: _____

_____

_____

I find it helpful when: _____

_____

_____

_____

I am comforted by: _____

_____

_____

_____

_____

I feel your presence most when: _____

_____

_____

Date: / /

If I need support today, I can call:

_____

My plans for today include:

_____

_____

_____

Today, I'm really missing:

_____

_____

_____

If you were here, I would tell you: _____

_____

_____

I find it helpful when: _____

_____

_____

_____

I am comforted by: _____

_____

_____

_____

_____

I feel your presence most when: _____

_____

_____

Today I:
☐ Feel supported
☐ Feel angry
☐ Feel like crying
☐ Feel tired
☐ Feel sad
☐ Feel neutral
☐ Am taking it minute by minute

Date: /   /

If I need support today, I can call:

_____

My plans for today include:

_____

_____

_____

Today, I'm really missing:

_____

_____

_____

If you were here, I would tell you: _____

_____

_____

I find it helpful when: _____

_____

_____

_____

I am comforted by: _____

_____

_____

_____

_____

I feel your presence most when: _____

_____

_____

Today I:
☐ Feel supported
☐ Feel angry
☐ Feel like crying
☐ Feel tired
☐ Feel sad
☐ Feel neutral
☐ Am taking it minute by minute

Date: / /

If I need support today, I can call:

_____

My plans for today include:

_____

_____

_____

Today, I'm really missing:

_____

_____

_____

If you were here, I would tell you: _____

_____

_____

I find it helpful when: _____

_____

_____

_____

I am comforted by: _____

_____

_____

_____

_____

I feel your presence most when: _____

_____

_____

Today I:
- ☐ Feel supported
- ☐ Feel angry
- ☐ Feel like crying
- ☐ Feel tired
- ☐ Feel sad
- ☐ Feel neutral
- ☐ Am taking it minute by minute

Date: /   /

If I need support today, I can call:

_____

My plans for today include:

_____

_____

_____

Today, I'm really missing:

Today I:
- ☐ Feel supported
- ☐ Feel angry
- ☐ Feel like crying
- ☐ Feel tired
- ☐ Feel sad
- ☐ Feel neutral
- ☐ Am taking it minute by minute

_____

_____

_____

If you were here, I would tell you: _____

_____

_____

I find it helpful when: _____

_____

_____

_____

I am comforted by: _____

_____

_____

_____

_____

I feel your presence most when: _____

_____

_____

Date: / /

If I need support today, I can call:

_____

My plans for today include:

_____

_____

_____

Today, I'm really missing:

Today I:
- ☐ Feel supported
- ☐ Feel angry
- ☐ Feel like crying
- ☐ Feel tired
- ☐ Feel sad
- ☐ Feel neutral
- ☐ Am taking it minute by minute

_____

_____

_____

If you were here, I would tell you: _____

_____

_____

I find it helpful when: _____

_____

_____

_____

I am comforted by: _____

_____

_____

_____

_____

I feel your presence most when: _____

_____

_____

Date: /   /

If I need support today, I can call:

_____

My plans for today include:

_____

_____

_____

Today, I'm really missing:

_____

_____

_____

If you were here, I would tell you: _____

_____

_____

I find it helpful when: _____

_____

_____

_____

I am comforted by: _____

_____

_____

_____

_____

I feel your presence most when: _____

_____

_____

Date: ___/___/___

If I need support today, I can call:

_____

My plans for today include:

_____

_____

_____

Today, I'm really missing:

_____

_____

_____

If you were here, I would tell you: _____

_____

_____

I find it helpful when: _____

_____

_____

_____

I am comforted by: _____

_____

_____

_____

_____

I feel your presence most when: _____

_____

_____

Today I:
- ☐ Feel supported
- ☐ Feel angry
- ☐ Feel like crying
- ☐ Feel tired
- ☐ Feel sad
- ☐ Feel neutral
- ☐ Am taking it minute by minute

Date: /   /

If I need support today, I can call:

_____

My plans for today include:

_____

_____

_____

Today, I'm really missing:

Today I:
- ☐ Feel supported
- ☐ Feel angry
- ☐ Feel like crying
- ☐ Feel tired
- ☐ Feel sad
- ☐ Feel neutral
- ☐ Am taking it minute by minute

_____

_____

_____

If you were here, I would tell you: _____

_____

_____

I find it helpful when: _____

_____

_____

_____

I am comforted by: _____

_____

_____

_____

_____

I feel your presence most when: _____

_____

_____

Date: ___ / ___ / ___

If I need support today, I can call:

_____

My plans for today include:

_____

_____

_____

Today, I'm really missing:

_____

_____

_____

If you were here, I would tell you: _____

_____

_____

I find it helpful when: _____

_____

_____

_____

I am comforted by: _____

_____

_____

_____

_____

I feel your presence most when: _____

_____

_____

Today I:
- ☐ Feel supported
- ☐ Feel angry
- ☐ Feel like crying
- ☐ Feel tired
- ☐ Feel sad
- ☐ Feel neutral
- ☐ Am taking it minute by minute

Date: / /

If I need support today, I can call:

_____

My plans for today include:

_____

_____

_____

Today, I'm really missing:

_____

_____

_____

If you were here, I would tell you: _____

_____

_____

I find it helpful when: _____

_____

_____

_____

I am comforted by: _____

_____

_____

_____

_____

I feel your presence most when: _____

_____

_____

Today I:
☐ Feel supported
☐ Feel angry
☐ Feel like crying
☐ Feel tired
☐ Feel sad
☐ Feel neutral
☐ Am taking it
minute by minute

Date: / /

If I need support today, I can call:

_____

My plans for today include:

_____

_____

_____

Today, I'm really missing:

_____

_____

_____

If you were here, I would tell you: _____

_____

_____

I find it helpful when: _____

_____

_____

_____

I am comforted by: _____

_____

_____

_____

_____

I feel your presence most when: _____

_____

_____

Today I:
☐ Feel supported
☐ Feel angry
☐ Feel like crying
☐ Feel tired
☐ Feel sad
☐ Feel neutral
☐ Am taking it minute by minute

Date: /   /

If I need support today, I can call:

_____

My plans for today include:

_____

_____

_____

Today, I'm really missing:

_____

_____

_____

If you were here, I would tell you: _____

_____

_____

I find it helpful when: _____

_____

_____

_____

I am comforted by: _____

_____

_____

_____

I feel your presence most when: _____

_____

_____

Today I:
- ☐ Feel supported
- ☐ Feel angry
- ☐ Feel like crying
- ☐ Feel tired
- ☐ Feel sad
- ☐ Feel neutral
- ☐ Am taking it minute by minute

Date: /   /

If I need support today, I can call:

_____

My plans for today include:

_____

_____

_____

Today, I'm really missing:

Today I:
- ☐ Feel supported
- ☐ Feel angry
- ☐ Feel like crying
- ☐ Feel tired
- ☐ Feel sad
- ☐ Feel neutral
- ☐ Am taking it minute by minute

_____

_____

_____

If you were here, I would tell you: _____

_____

_____

I find it helpful when: _____

_____

_____

_____

I am comforted by: _____

_____

_____

_____

_____

I feel your presence most when: _____

_____

_____

Date: /   /

If I need support today, I can call:

_____

My plans for today include:

_____

_____

_____

Today, I'm really missing:

Today I:

☐ Feel supported
☐ Feel angry
☐ Feel like crying
☐ Feel tired
☐ Feel sad
☐ Feel neutral
☐ Am taking it minute by minute

_____

_____

_____

If you were here, I would tell you: _____

_____

I find it helpful when: _____

_____

_____

I am comforted by: _____

_____

_____

_____

I feel your presence most when: _____

_____

_____

Date: /   /

If I need support today, I can call:

_____

My plans for today include:

_____

_____

_____

Today, I'm really missing:

Today I:
- ☐ Feel supported
- ☐ Feel angry
- ☐ Feel like crying
- ☐ Feel tired
- ☐ Feel sad
- ☐ Feel neutral
- ☐ Am taking it minute by minute

_____

_____

_____

If you were here, I would tell you: _____

_____

_____

I find it helpful when: _____

_____

_____

I am comforted by: _____

_____

_____

_____

I feel your presence most when: _____

_____

_____

Date: /   /

If I need support today, I can call:

_____

My plans for today include:

_____

_____

_____

Today, I'm really missing:

Today I:
☐ Feel supported
☐ Feel angry
☐ Feel like crying
☐ Feel tired
☐ Feel sad
☐ Feel neutral
☐ Am taking it minute by minute

_____

_____

_____

If you were here, I would tell you: _____

_____

_____

I find it helpful when: _____

_____

_____

_____

I am comforted by: _____

_____

_____

_____

_____

I feel your presence most when: _____

_____

_____

Date: / /

If I need support today, I can call:

_____

My plans for today include:

_____

_____

_____

Today, I'm really missing:

_____

_____

_____

If you were here, I would tell you: _____

_____

_____

I find it helpful when: _____

_____

_____

_____

I am comforted by: _____

_____

_____

_____

_____

I feel your presence most when: _____

_____

_____

Today I:
☐ Feel supported
☐ Feel angry
☐ Feel like crying
☐ Feel tired
☐ Feel sad
☐ Feel neutral
☐ Am taking it minute by minute

Date: /   /

If I need support today, I can call:

_____

My plans for today include:

_____

_____

_____

Today, I'm really missing:

Today I:
- ☐ Feel supported
- ☐ Feel angry
- ☐ Feel like crying
- ☐ Feel tired
- ☐ Feel sad
- ☐ Feel neutral
- ☐ Am taking it minute by minute

_____

_____

_____

If you were here, I would tell you: _____

_____

_____

I find it helpful when: _____

_____

_____

_____

I am comforted by: _____

_____

_____

_____

_____

I feel your presence most when: _____

_____

_____

Date: / /

If I need support today, I can call:

_____

My plans for today include:

_____

_____

_____

Today, I'm really missing:

_____

_____

_____

If you were here, I would tell you: _____

_____

_____

I find it helpful when: _____

_____

_____

_____

I am comforted by: _____

_____

_____

_____

_____

I feel your presence most when: _____

_____

_____

Today I:
- ☐ Feel supported
- ☐ Feel angry
- ☐ Feel like crying
- ☐ Feel tired
- ☐ Feel sad
- ☐ Feel neutral
- ☐ Am taking it minute by minute

Date: /   /

If I need support today, I can call:

_____

My plans for today include:

_____

_____

_____

Today, I'm really missing:

_____

_____

_____

If you were here, I would tell you: _____

_____

_____

I find it helpful when: _____

_____

_____

_____

I am comforted by: _____

_____

_____

_____

_____

I feel your presence most when: _____

_____

_____

Date: /   /

If I need support today, I can call:

_____

My plans for today include:

_____

_____

_____

Today, I'm really missing:

Today I:
- ☐ Feel supported
- ☐ Feel angry
- ☐ Feel like crying
- ☐ Feel tired
- ☐ Feel sad
- ☐ Feel neutral
- ☐ Am taking it minute by minute

_____

_____

_____

If you were here, I would tell you: _____

_____

_____

I find it helpful when: _____

_____

_____

_____

I am comforted by: _____

_____

_____

_____

I feel your presence most when: _____

_____

_____

Date: /   /

If I need support today, I can call:

_____

My plans for today include:

_____

_____

_____

Today, I'm really missing:

<table>
<tr><td>Today I:</td></tr>
</table>

Today I:
☐ Feel supported
☐ Feel angry
☐ Feel like crying
☐ Feel tired
☐ Feel sad
☐ Feel neutral
☐ Am taking it minute by minute

_____

_____

_____

If you were here, I would tell you: _____

_____

_____

I find it helpful when: _____

_____

_____

_____

I am comforted by: _____

_____

_____

_____

_____

I feel your presence most when: _____

_____

_____

Date: / /

If I need support today, I can call:

_____

My plans for today include:

_____

_____

_____

Today, I'm really missing:

_____

_____

_____

If you were here, I would tell you: _____

_____

_____

I find it helpful when: _____

_____

_____

_____

I am comforted by: _____

_____

_____

_____

_____

I feel your presence most when: _____

_____

_____

Today I:
☐ Feel supported
☐ Feel angry
☐ Feel like crying
☐ Feel tired
☐ Feel sad
☐ Feel neutral
☐ Am taking it minute by minute

Date: /   /

If I need support today, I can call:

_____

My plans for today include:

_____

_____

_____

Today, I'm really missing:

☐ Feel supported
☐ Feel angry
☐ Feel like crying
☐ Feel tired
☐ Feel sad
☐ Feel neutral
☐ Am taking it minute by minute

_____

_____

_____

If you were here, I would tell you: _____

_____

_____

I find it helpful when: _____

_____

_____

_____

I am comforted by: _____

_____

_____

_____

_____

I feel your presence most when: _____

_____

_____

Date: /   /

If I need support today, I can call:

_____

My plans for today include:

_____

_____

_____

Today, I'm really missing:

Today I:
- ☐ Feel supported
- ☐ Feel angry
- ☐ Feel like crying
- ☐ Feel tired
- ☐ Feel sad
- ☐ Feel neutral
- ☐ Am taking it minute by minute

_____

_____

_____

If you were here, I would tell you: _____

_____

I find it helpful when: _____

_____

_____

I am comforted by: _____

_____

_____

_____

I feel your presence most when: _____

_____

_____

Date: /   /

If I need support today, I can call:

_____

My plans for today include:

_____

_____

_____

Today, I'm really missing:

Today I:
☐ Feel supported
☐ Feel angry
☐ Feel like crying
☐ Feel tired
☐ Feel sad
☐ Feel neutral
☐ Am taking it minute by minute

_____

_____

_____

If you were here, I would tell you: _____

_____

_____

I find it helpful when: _____

_____

_____

_____

I am comforted by: _____

_____

_____

_____

_____

I feel your presence most when: _____

_____

_____

Date: /   /

If I need support today, I can call:

_____

My plans for today include:

_____

_____

_____

Today, I'm really missing:

Today I:
☐ Feel supported
☐ Feel angry
☐ Feel like crying
☐ Feel tired
☐ Feel sad
☐ Feel neutral
☐ Am taking it
minute by minute

_____

_____

_____

If you were here, I would tell you: _____

_____

_____

I find it helpful when: _____

_____

_____

_____

I am comforted by: _____

_____

_____

_____

I feel your presence most when: _____

_____

_____

Date: /   /

If I need support today, I can call:

_____

My plans for today include:

_____

_____

_____

Today, I'm really missing:

Today I:
☐ Feel supported
☐ Feel angry
☐ Feel like crying
☐ Feel tired
☐ Feel sad
☐ Feel neutral
☐ Am taking it minute by minute

_____

_____

_____

If you were here, I would tell you: _____

_____

_____

I find it helpful when: _____

_____

_____

_____

I am comforted by: _____

_____

_____

_____

_____

I feel your presence most when: _____

_____

_____

Date: /   /

If I need support today, I can call:

_____

My plans for today include:

_____

_____

_____

Today, I'm really missing:

Today I:

☐ Feel supported
☐ Feel angry
☐ Feel like crying
☐ Feel tired
☐ Feel sad
☐ Feel neutral
☐ Am taking it minute by minute

_____

_____

_____

If you were here, I would tell you: _____

_____

_____

I find it helpful when: _____

_____

_____

_____

I am comforted by: _____

_____

_____

_____

_____

I feel your presence most when: _____

_____

_____

114

Date: /   /

If I need support today, I can call:

_____

My plans for today include:

_____

_____

_____

Today, I'm really missing:

Today I:
☐ Feel supported
☐ Feel angry
☐ Feel like crying
☐ Feel tired
☐ Feel sad
☐ Feel neutral
☐ Am taking it minute by minute

_____

_____

_____

If you were here, I would tell you: _____

_____

_____

I find it helpful when: _____

_____

_____

_____

I am comforted by: _____

_____

_____

_____

I feel your presence most when: _____

_____

_____

I will honor your legacy by:

_____

_____

_____

_____

_____

_____

_____

_____

_____

_____

_____

_____

_____

_____

_____

_____

_____

_____

I will honor your legacy by:

_____

_____

_____

_____

_____

_____

_____

_____

_____

_____

_____

_____

_____

_____

_____

_____

_____

I will honor your legacy by:

_____

_____

_____

_____

_____

_____

_____

_____

_____

_____

_____

_____

_____

_____

_____

_____

_____

_____

_____

_____

25 WAYS TO KEEP YOUR LOVED ONE'S SPIRIT ALIVE AFTER THEY HAVE TRANSITIONED

Over the years, I've witnessed family members and friends transition. And often, after the funeral, not too many words are spoken about the departed except during special occasions that may prompt a memory or two from time to time.

I have come to learn through my experiences, that people grieve their loss in different ways.

For some, the loss is so painful that they are unable to discuss it.

For others, the decedent died before asking for forgiveness and repairing broken relationships. In some families the decedent may have been an abusive or otherwise horrible person that quite frankly people are more at peace with their non-existence than they were when they were among the living.

There are those remaining family members that want to keep their loved one's spirit alive but may be afraid that they will be seen as "not letting go" or "not moving on" so instead they secretly pine away on the inside and brokenhearted while missing their departed loved one.

Then there are people like me, an only child of a single mother who has no blood relatives or parents -- besides me. In light of this fact, I exert the same level of responsibility, love, and care shown to her while she was living, in her death.

I want to do everything in my power to honor her spirit, keep her memories alive and to educate others about her legacy. Her, being my mother, Beverly E. Carroll who suddenly and unexpectedly passed away in October 2018.

There's no blueprint on how to remember your loved one, and there is no requirement to do so - it's an individual choice.

For those that share similar views as I do about keeping your loved one's memory alive, or if you've lost a loved one and you want to know how you can keep their memory alive, I've compiled a list of 25 ways to keep your loved one's spirit alive after they have transitioned.

1. Talk about your loved one daily
2. Write down your thoughts about your loved one as they occur to you
3. Record your dreams about your departed loved one
4. Wear their favorite color
5. Dine at their favorite restaurant on a special occasion
6. Memorialize and update their social media pages
7. Plant a tree
8. Organize a balloon release on special occasions
9. Visit their final resting spot frequently
10. Stay in contact with your loved one's closest friends and exchange memories
11. Create photo pillows and blankets with their image
12. Complete things they wanted to complete but they did not complete (I wrote and released a published book because my mom always wanted to be a published author)
13. Create and maintain a garden of their favorite fruits or vegetables
14. Honor their spirit during special occasions by placing a single rose in a chair honoring their spiritual presence
15. Celebrate /Acknowledge their heavenly birthdays
16. Commit Random Acts of Kindness

17. Create social media groups & exchange memories with others who have lost loved ones

18. Burn their favorite scented candles

19. Create a sacred box that includes precious items of your loved one

20. Name your child after your loved one

21. Go on a vacation that your loved one always wanted to go on

22. Walk on the beach barefoot and allow beautiful memories to flow about your loved one

23. Donate to their favorite charity/organization

24. Ask their favorite employer to create and hang a memorial plaque

25. Wear jewelry that reminds you of your loved one (I wear bee jewelry to feel close to my mom's spirit since I always called her Miss Bee)

Again, there is no right or wrong way to honor your loved one's legacy or how to keep their spirit alive.

I'm sharing this information with those who may be inspired to keep their loved one's spirit alive.

Creating this grief journal is another why I have chosen to honor the legacy of my mother, Miss Bee.

Whatever you do, don't abandon their spirit.

Kinyatta E. Gray is a published author of four books that can be found on her website **kinyattagray.com** she is also the CEO of **FlightsInStilettos, LLC** (flightsinstilettos.com).

Disclaimer: Kinyatta Gray is not a mental health provider and is providing this information based on real-life experience and to inspire others to keep their loved one's legacy alive. If you are experiencing a physical or emotional crisis, seek the help of a mental health professional.

I miss you. I love you. I'm taking it day by day for as long as it takes.

Kinyatta E. Gray

AUTHOR & CELEBRITY TRAVEL INFLUENCER

CPSIA information can be obtained
at www.ICGtesting.com
Printed in the USA
BVHW050050301021
619793BV00002B/3